HANGING BY A THREAD

Survival Guide for Blacks in Corporate America

by

Lisa Brown

authorHOUSE®

AuthorHouse™
1663 Liberty Drive, Suite 200
Bloomington, IN 47403
www.authorhouse.com
Phone: 1-800-839-8640

First published by AuthorHouse 2/27/2008

ISBN: 978-1-4343-2693-5 (sc)

Printed in the United States of America
Bloomington, Indiana

This book is printed on acid-free paper.

Contents

ACKNOWLEDGEMENTS

I am deeply indebted to Harriet Wilkes for her patience and writing coaching. Without her keen insight and talent, this book would not have materialized. I would also like to thank Karen S. Williams for encouraging my dream and affirming that I should take my publishing destiny into my own hands. My thanks also go to Karen Celestan for reading and giving me feedback on my writing. Thank you to "Dr. Durham" for your insistence that the voice of black professionals trying to survive in corporate America needs to be heard. I would also like to thank my mother for exposing me to books she had in her library at a historically black college, books about people who look like me. My appreciation also goes to my father for pushing the book. I would specially like to thank Robert Aulicino for creating a wonderful and striking cover. Finally, I give thanks to God for channeling the ideas and outline for this book long before it was written.

INTRODUCTION

If you are looking for a phony, politically correct book, you had better put this one down. This guide is written as a voice for the person who often doesn't have one or whose voice is rarely heard: *the black corporate employee*. What makes me an expert on this subject? I'm not a Ph.D., M.D., or J.D., but I do have a graduate degree and have worked for four Fortune 500 companies. I also have black professional associates in engineering, information technology, financial services, marketing, and the medical industry. No matter where we go, the same messed-up work scenarios continue to haunt us. Why do all these people seem to have the same problems? Racism knows no education or income level — and in the workplace, it is more subtle and harder to handle. By the time most of us learn to read the political roadmap at work, we have been demoted or laid off.

Today's corporate workplace can be very dirty. Along with hard work and improved technology, frequent organizational changes and backstabbing are common. These roadblocks create a difficult environment for today's black professional to navigate.

In an interview with the *Milwaukee Journal Sentinel* in March 2005, networking guru George Fraser said, "At least 60 percent of the black workforce — nine million people — is in executive, managerial, supervisory, professional specialty, vocational, technical, administrative, sales, and business ownership positions." This data reveals that many blacks are employed in the professional and executive ranks. Quite often, however, blacks are not in the right "political circles" to gain access to information early enough. Consequently, they suffer career damage in corporate America.

To top it off, blacks are no longer the "hot" minority. The Hispanic population has increased considerably, with the most striking growth in Texas, California, and Florida. As a result, companies are scurrying to recruit and market to this population.

Del Clark, community development project manager for Georgia Power, said in a July 2006 interview with the *Atlanta Journal-Constitution*, "The Hispanic community is our fastest-growing customer base, and we strive to mirror our base and be a good citizen wherever we serve. We're competing with every other company for bilingual employees; it's a hot employment topic."

The corporate landscape has changed; we, as professional blacks, need more effective ways to survive on the job.

Blacks create informal networks of support because traditional organizations sometimes supply impractical or outdated advice. Inside the workplace, human resources departments are required to take a safe, often ineffective stance on difficult issues; therefore, they offer little help. This forces black professionals to seek other avenues of support. African American professional organizations have many members at the same level who themselves may be struggling. These groups often turn into social clubs, planning events to keep members from feeling isolated away from their jobs. We also talk to our mothers, grandmothers, and friends about how to deal with problems at work. Though they mean well, these people may give bad advice because some of them have never worked in high-level corporate jobs. The best they can do is make up something to tell you. It's time to take the whispered advice mainstream and keep it real. Whether we like it or not, the rules in the work trenches differ if you are black.

Contrary to popular belief, many black professionals are hanging by a thread. Why are so many black professionals facing danger? Unless you are in the super minority of black people who have a trust fund, you have to work somewhere to pay your bills. Some single black professionals support only themselves financially; others may have a primary family to support as well as a secondary family such as mother, father, or children from a prior relationship. Additional financial burdens may intensify the fear of job loss.

The purpose of this book is to give you practical strategies for dealing with some of the most treacherous work situations. In my seventeen years of experience in corporate America, I have witnessed circumstances that keep us immobile. Review each of the following questions. If these are things that you have experienced, then this book is for you.

Compensation: Did you settle for an unfair salary coming in the door? Were you running from another job during your hiring process, and negotiating from a position of desperation? Now that you're in the company, have your promotions and raises been slow to nonexistent?

Help at Home: Do you have help at home? Are you in direct competition with white males who have a stay-at-home wife or white females who can afford domestic help?

Geographical Disadvantage: Do you live in the same neighborhood and go to church together with your white counterparts? Do your kids attend school and sporting events alongside theirs? They may have opportunities to network and build alliances outside of work to which you don't have access.

Subtle Bias: Do you get the feeling that your white manager is spending more time coaching and grooming your white peers? A co-worker or subordinate may remind him of a sister, mother, wife, son, or daughter. White managers may feel they have to spend too much time trying to figure us out. People of all races and genders gravitate toward, and open up to, people with whom they feel comfortable. This may be due to a theory called "unconscious bias" coined by sociologist William Bielby, which states that white men will inevitably slight women and minorities because they just can't help themselves.

No Financial Leverage: Do you have some financial concerns that mentally de-energize you? White Americans are usually better off financially. They have more assets and less debt. The Center for Responsible Lending reported that black households had a median net worth of $5,988 in 2002, compared with $88,651 for white households. Financial stress impedes your ability to think and advance at work. Therefore, most of the time, you will be at a disadvantage.

Promotion Euphoria: Have you known blacks who received promotions and then seemed to lose their competitive edge while basking in the glow of their success? The higher the level to which you are promoted, the tougher the games become. A little success at work can spell potential doom for you because you have more people eyeing your job. Some of us are too busy patting ourselves on the back, which makes it easier for us to be picked off.

Big Daddy, White Daddy: How do you know you are listening to the right people? Are you getting advice from family members or black mentors who themselves are hanging by a thread? These people can share little advice to help you fight the nasty war you are in. An older, successful white male may be the best bet for a mentor, but few of us obtain one. Female mentors are excellent, but there are not as many to choose from in the highest executive positions. Ken Chenault, CEO of American Express, and Oprah Winfrey, reigning queen of the talk show circuit, are two examples of African Americans who achieved groundbreaking success in their fields because they had powerful white male mentors who gave them access to unique opportunities, as well as critical information. For them, the white mentors provided the turning point in their career.

Big-Head Syndrome: Did you roll out of an Ivy League college or HBCU thinking you could conquer the world? Some of us think that if we are educated at Ivy League or historically black colleges, we can say whatever is on our mind as we did in the open school environment. Wrong! Did you know that this thinking could get you isolated and ostracized by your white manager quicker than anything? Have you noticed that he or she might have a team of congenial, capable white men and women who are ready to run with your high-profile projects?

Being Pimped: As a black female, do you feel you work harder for less money than your counterparts because your personal life is lacking? Have you fallen into the trap of letting a charming manager suck the life out of you at work just because you are starved for praise and accept rewards of a few low raises and token promotions?

Single Life: Are you single or divorced? Did you know that blacks remain single longer? In August 2005, The Joint Center Data Bank conducted a study, "Marriage and African Americans". The study revealed that "the percentage of African American women who are married declined from 62 percent to 36.1 percent between 1950 and 2000. Among white women, the corresponding decline was from 66 percent to 57.4 percent." The study goes on to say, "In 1990, black men (75.8 marriages per thousand) were much less likely than white men (119.2 per thousand) to marry for the first time between ages 25 and 29, but were somewhat more likely to marry between ages 40 and 44 (31.9 for black men compared to 29.7 for white men) and after age 45." Being partnered up can translate to less stress and more stability, which in turn can mean higher productivity at work.

I have gathered actual stories that represent common situations blacks experience in the corporate world, as well as strategies to prevent these problems. These are recommendations that may sound hardcore, but they work. We need practical, no-nonsense navigation techniques to keep us from continuing to be casualties in the workplace.

Chapter 1:

THE ULTIMATE IN CORPORATE SURVIVAL — WORK GODFATHER

Everyone remembers the famous movie *The Godfather*. In the movie, the Godfather established businesses in certain neighborhoods. He had loyal sons and lieutenants running those businesses for him. In turn, he provided them with a good standard of living and protection. Turf battles would break out, but the Godfather always expected loyalty from his "troops".

The "Godfather" relationship is not limited to the streets. Most successful blacks who have risen to the top of the corporate ranks had protection from senior executives. There are two ways that I have seen blacks obtain a "Work Godfather":

1. A manager hires a black employee who displays great potential. The two of them click. The manager trusts the employee and moves him/her up the corporate

ladder with him. Manager rises; black employee rises.

2. Senior manager hires a black employee from outside of the corporation. The manager provides the employee with a cloak of protection. The fact that a high-level executive brought the black employee into the company immediately scares off some of the employee's potential enemies.

During a black employee's ascent through the management ranks, there will always be people who have their eyes on his position. The relationship between the black employee and his manager can provoke jealousy among insecure white colleagues. This alone can fuel their plans to take out the black employee. These same white colleagues may be inclined to think that they are more qualified, thus believing they deserve his position. Once the white colleagues feel this way, they have little conscience when they begin poisoning the black employee's reputation. They do this through small but well-placed negative comments about the black employee to his manager. If this subtle sabotage continues, perception about the black employee may change. Soon the black employee begins to suffer aggressive attacks relating to his effectiveness. Unfortunately, these games often succeed because they are invariably played behind the black employee's back, in the darkness and casual anonymity of after-work drinking sessions or in meetings he can't attend or to which he is not invited.

There is only one person who can save a black employee from a serious case of reputation poisoning: the Work Godfather. When an enemy attacks the employee head on, the employee picks up the phone and schedules a meeting with Work Godfather. Because the black employee has formed an alliance with Work Godfather's secretary in the past, she's receptive to scheduling the meeting immediately. Ordinarily, the black employee would have scheduled a meeting to discuss his achievements with Work Godfather. However, this time the black employee has a problem to discuss. Ideally, after such a meeting, the Work Godfather will immediately pick up the phone and call the enemy's manager. This will scare the crap out of the enemy's manager because the manager will not want to alienate the powerful Work Godfather. In the short term, the enemy's manager will call the enemy to his office, question his tactics, and reprimand him. Shaken and humbled, the enemy will retreat.

Karen cultivated the Work Godfather relationship. She was hired by a powerful good ol' boy at a large Fortune 500 company who saw her potential. He always praised all of her accomplishments, even though she was at a lower level. Eventually, he moved on to a much higher position. Karen continued to work faithfully in her old role. She always made sure she placed a phone call to her hiring manager to let him know how she was doing. He continued up the corporate ladder until he ran all locations in the Canadian market.

Karen began working under a new manager, Christopher, who came in with a lot of energy and ambition. He was willing to sell his grandma to get ahead, and his style of employee motivation was to pit one employee against another. When Karen resisted these underhanded tactics, Christopher became displeased with her. He reassigned her to junk projects and reduced her visibility. Karen felt Christopher was jealous of some of the credit his peers were giving her on projects well done. He continued to accelerate his effort to limit her work, and even commented that she was too articulate and poised. Karen felt threatened and feared for her job. She did what a smart employee would do – she called her Work Godfather and explained the situation to him. Based on their history of working together, Work Godfather knew Karen was trustworthy. He picked up the phone, called her black mentor, and told him what he was going to do. They both called Christopher and had a conversation with him. Christopher lightened up on Karen but made her aware that he had received some phone calls. He wanted to know how she knew these executives. Karen gave him a little information but did not reveal the extent of her alliances. Without Work Godfather, Christopher would have discredited Karen and laid her off.

Jealous co-workers and managers often create situations that will cause you to need the help of your Work Godfather.

Now, let's meet Sherry, a twenty-something black employee who was pursuing a job change in human resources. With the job change, her salary should have been in the low six figures. Her potential manager, Hilda, was an older black female who had told Sherry she hadn't made that kind of money when she was Sherry's age. She offered her a raise that was half what Sherry should have been given with the position, and it would keep her below six figures. Sherry tried to have a heart-to-heart talk with Hilda to express her viewpoint, but Hilda had made up her mind. Sherry felt stifled and began to look for jobs outside the company. When she landed a job that offered considerably more than she had asked from her current employer, Hilda came back with a lower counteroffer. Sherry became frustrated and went to talk to her Work Godfather. He was an older, established white male who had appointed the current CEO. He and his colleague called Hilda to pressure her to pay Sherry fairly. Due to a fear of political ramifications, Hilda relented and offered Sherry the salary she deserved.

Unfortunately, a black employee can start out with a Work Godfather and lose him. Such was the case with Willie, a merger and acquisition specialist from New York. Willie wasn't too keen on moving his family south, but would consider it for the right opportunity. The CEO of a large corporation, let's call him Henry, spent personal time recruiting Willie to his company. He recognized Willie's stellar credentials, and urged him to become part of his growing company. Willie acknowledged this as a great opportunity for advancement, so he and his family relocated. He was placed in a senior executive position in a growing division. Henry looked out for Willie and ensured that he was compensated handsomely. However, Henry had spent many years building the company and felt the need to retire two years after Willie had joined. A new president came in and Willie lost his Work Godfather's influence. He was progressively demoted to positions with less responsibility. Sadly enough, Work Godfather's departure, coupled with Willie's demotions, left Willie hanging on by a thread. Without the protection of his Work Godfather, Willie was unable to display his skills and advance. He was pushed to no-man's-land and is worried about what his fate will be in the next big reorganization. The upside of this scenario is that Willie was smart enough to funnel his earnings into outside business ventures. He capitalized on his passion for sports, and invested in an opportunity to become co-manager of a sports team.

Perhaps the epitome of the Work Godfather relationship is the connection between Condoleezza Rice and President George W.

Bush. Even though she is highly qualified and speaks five languages, her opponents questioned her political stance on the war in Iraq. During hearings examining the U.S. participation in the war, she was intensely questioned about her decisions to send troops overseas. Everyone knew these decisions were based on so-called "weapons of mass destruction." Whenever the Democrats tried to discredit her, President Bush came to her defense. Her enemies were forced to withdraw, leaving Condoleezza in her powerful role. She went on about her business of being Secretary of State. George Bush chose her because she is smart and loyal. He could not have gotten better performance from a white Secretary of State, and he knows it. Even though Condoleezza Rice is prominent and highly astute, she still benefits from having a Work Godfather.

The lucky few who have a Work Godfather have a protective cloak that deflects games that aim to eliminate or discredit. A Work Godfather is the ultimate weapon of survival for a black in corporate America.

Chapter 2:

THE WHITE MALE'S ULTIMATE WEAPON —
WORK WIFE, HOME WIFE

Everyone's heard the cliché "behind every great man is a great woman." However, most people are not familiar with who is behind most successful corporate men: a Work Wife and a Home Wife. In general, "wives" tend to have things in common. They collaborate, help with tasks, and provide stability to the husband's world. They take care of other people — kids, or co-workers. Importantly, they are cheerleaders for their man.

Building alliances in the workplace is critical. White males have been playing the corporate game longer than anyone and are quite adept at generating support. Often, a white male who is successful and pulling down a large income has the luxury of having a stay-at-home wife. She does the shopping, household errands, cooking, and caring for his children. I think one mistake the women's liberation movement made was to devalue and undermine the impact of these women. When a male employee has most of his problems at home taken care of by a person he trusts, he can free his mind up to focus squarely on work in his eight-hour day. He is also not spending his precious spare time trying to generate a social life in order to meet a life partner. In the stay-at-home wife scenario, the gender may change, but the concept remains the same. Remember *Family Affair*, the 1960s television show featuring a single white father who had to care for three kids? He gained custody of a teenager and a set of young twins. His hectic schedule of managing his new flock, coupled with his business trips, household tasks, and busy dating life, compelled Uncle Bill to get stay-at-home help. However, there was a unique spin on how he remedied his problem. Instead of getting married, he hired a butler, Mr. French, who was a miracle worker. He not only cooked, cleaned, and dressed the children, but he also gave advice to Uncle Bill. Having Mr. French at home reduced the burden of Uncle Bill's life as an executive.

Black female professionals, on the other hand, very rarely have a spouse who stays at home. Either she has a spouse who works but doesn't make enough money to maintain a certain lifestyle, or she does not have a spouse at all. No matter which scenario she falls in, the black professional woman is still usually expected to take care of all the duties of the home front as well as work hard at her job.

A situation black female professionals often find themselves in is playing Work Wife to a white professional male. She may be assigned to deliver on his key projects because he can count on her. She provides him insight and ideas that he may not have thought about. He confides in her about his work enemies. His way of rewarding her for her loyalty can vary, from good reviews and consistent raises to moving her along with him as he advances.

George had a Work Wife in Tameka. George had been an employee at a Fortune 500 company for many years. He was part of a new, key initiative that the company was rolling out. He needed to hire talent with the experience that he lacked. He interviewed Tameka for the first spot on his new team. She was articulate, experienced, but above all a warm person with whom he felt comfortable. He hired Tameka, giving her his largest project. She assembled the team, detailed the deliverables, and drove them to execution. When George reported status to upper-level management, he was not only ahead of schedule but also under budget.

Tameka expended most of her energy at work. She found it difficult to develop a social life. Too much of her time was devoted to driving her co-workers to deliver. Unfortunately, one way she chose to wind down was indulging in high-fat foods. While George went home to healthy, home-cooked meals his wife prepared, Tameka would be pulling up to a drive-through window on her way home.

Even though George was getting the better end of the deal, Tameka asked for and received hefty bonuses and good performance reviews. They had a partnership that seemed to work for both of them.

Why would this scenario be a problem for the black professional woman? First, Tameka should not have devoted so much time to her job at the expense of everything else. She needed the same type of support at home that her manager had. She needed a place where she could be revitalized and nurtured. Without such support, two questions come to mind: What would happen if her manager quit or transferred to another role? What would happen if she was laid off? Obviously, Tameka would have no support system at home to help her recover.

Sometimes the white male manager knows that the black professional woman does not have a life and often uses this to his advantage. Gail, a workaholic, found herself in this predicament. She worked as a behind-the-scenes person for her manager, Philippe. Philippe could always rely on her to create presentations and projects. Dressed in his expensive custom-tailored suits, he would then take her hard work and go present it to upper-level management. Top management thought Philippe was a genius, and based on his stellar results, he was soon promoted.

Philippe was a charmer. He used this skill to his advantage, often flattering Gail to work even harder. He knew she was single with no man in sight, and was more than willing to stroke Gail's ego because he knew she was starved for male attention. In turn, he received a huge output of work from Gail that impressed his superiors. However, this did not prevent Philippe from hiring younger, cuter blondes for his staff and paying them more than he did Gail, his tried-and-true performer. He used "pimp psychology" on Gail, and it worked to his advantage. Philippe earned three times Gail's salary by capitalizing on her hard work. He wasn't capable of doing this type of work alone.

Another way the Work Wife/Home Wife scenario plays out is with a white executive and his black secretary. Sharon fit this role perfectly. She was the secretary for an up-and-coming executive named Keith.

She always managed his calendar, deflecting nuisances from his workday. As Keith started climbing within the business, he took Sharon with him, since she always had his back. One day Keith was promoted to CEO and ensconced Sharon right by his side in the executive suite. Several white females already had their eyes set on Sharon's position. They failed at many of their tactics, including flirting with Keith, lying about Sharon, losing her memos, and ignoring her phone calls. Whenever Sharon felt like games were being played, she talked to Keith. He had known Sharon all these years. Having been around the block himself, he knew she wouldn't lie. He threatened retribution to those who gave Sharon a hard time and they immediately fell back in line. When Keith announced his retirement, he told Sharon that he was going to give her enough stock to retire as well. He didn't want to leave her behind for his enemies to devalue and humiliate. Unlike Tameka's situation, Sharon had both a Work Husband and a Home Husband. Sharon maintained a more balanced life because she had a supportive husband at home. Similarly, this worked for Keith as well. He had a Work Wife and a Home Wife.

Partnerships are necessary for a black female to make it in corporate America — as long as the support is mutually beneficial. Black females should not allow themselves to become victims of the sweet-talking Work Pimp. They should beware of such two-faced exploitation tactics; otherwise, the Work Pimp gets to keep his spouse in a luxurious, stay-at-home lifestyle at the Work Wife's expense. The black Work Wife needs to create balance in her life in order to prosper emotionally over the long run. Balance can come from a husband, boyfriend, or a supportive group of friends.

Chapter 3:

BLACK-ON-BLACK CRIME — MODERN HOUSE SLAVES

Mention the term "House Slave" to most black people and they will know exactly what you mean. During slavery, there were two types of slaves: House Slaves and Field Slaves. House Slaves were usually shown favoritism by the master — living in the house with him, receiving superior food, shelter, and clothing. This practice did not end with slavery. In corporate America, some black employees enjoy a favored status with white upper-level management. These blacks can represent modern House Slaves. Unfortunately, some white executives can spur competition between blacks who aspire to the coveted House Slave status. Sometimes this competition turns ugly, and results in black-on-black crime.

Tobias was a perpetrator of black-on-black crime. He had risen through the ranks of his company through his affiliation with an upper-level executive, Duncan. As a reward for years of loyalty,

Duncan promoted Tobias to be one of his direct reports. Tobias was offered a high salary and given considerable authority with his new position. No other black had risen to this level at the company. Tobias inherited his predecessor's twelve direct reports. Slowly, he replaced each of them with those he thought were loyal lieutenants. Tobias did not select any highly qualified blacks in the organization for his new team. He did not want to appear to be showing favoritism to his own kind, so he swung to the other extreme: He surrounded himself with hard-charging white males. In his mind, he thought they would get the job done and make him look good.

As time passed, management assigned Tobias greater goals. He trusted his staff and pushed the work down. He often went on the road, giving speeches and accepting awards on behalf of the company. Talk began to circulate that Tobias was an ineffective leader. His white direct reports were whispering that they did not feel he could take the division to the next level; he didn't have the passion of his predecessor.

Eventually, these rumblings floated up to his boss, Duncan, who listened to them with concern. He felt that there had to be some credence to them, because they came from multiple sources. He stripped most of Tobias' responsibilities and realigned him to a less powerful position. What was Tobias' mistake? Most savvy black managers will hire at least one black who they trust as part of their staff. This person can watch the manager's back and possibly give a heads-up on disloyal discussions by his peers.

If Tobias had been thinking, he would have cultivated alliances with some of the lower-level black managers. This would have helped him gain deeper intelligence regarding how he was perceived by the organization. Ultimately, the very people he tried to placate (white males) were the ones who took him down.

Black-on-black crime often occurs when a black manager is insecure about a new black professional coming onto the scene. Often, the black manager may feel that there is only room for one, and that *one* should be him. Christie was such an oppressive black manager. She reported to an aggressive and driven white female manager. Christie was smart, articulate, and hard-working. She always gave 150 percent to her assignments. Personnel did its job by sending diverse candidates to Christie. Several of these candidates were black females. Christie hired one black female after another for her team. However, none of them seemed to be able to survive under Christie's taskmaster leadership style. She often intimidated and disrespected them in one-on-one discussions, where this behavior couldn't be monitored by her white co-workers. One by one, each black female, after a short stint, transferred to another division. They shared stories about how nasty Christie had been to them. They all wondered how Christie could get away with treating them all so horribly. Later, management noticed that Christie could not maintain diversity among the employees despite the fact that she was black. In addition, Christie did not meet the goals specified in her performance plan. Management used this combination of failures as an opportunity to lay her off.

Some blacks who have survived at a company for years resent young black hires. They resent the fact that these new hires have shiny graduate degrees and nice salaries. Older blacks may feel that these young people have not paid their dues and should not be at the same level. Georgia was a senior black executive who resented Ashley.

Ashley was a young former consultant appointed to become part of Georgia's team. Eventually, Ashley requested a more prominent role on Georgia's team. Georgia agreed, but did not agree to the salary Ashley requested. She thought Ashley was too young to earn that salary, and told her so. Ashley ended up leaving Georgia's team and moving to another company, commanding an even higher salary than the one Georgia was unwilling to pay her.

A crafty move that is sometimes used by white management is to pit blacks against each other. Instead of getting rid of a troublesome black, they hire or promote another black to do the dirty work. This practice is comparable to how white slave owners used to employ a black overseer to keep the Field Slaves in check. This is a form of black-on-black crime set up by the system. Leslie was hired for her specific expertise from a well-known Fortune 500 company. She was excited about her new job with expanded responsibility. Leslie had a list of people to meet as part of her on-boarding plan. One of the managers scheduled to meet Leslie was Angela, another black female. Leslie was impressed with Angela's knowledge and her attitude, but did not find out that she was supposed to replace Angela until the end of her first week. Leslie did not feel right about taking a position from another black female. She extended an olive branch to Angela, explaining the situation as she perceived it. Angela was too defensive to form an alliance, continuing to fight to retain her power. Both women ended up being the losers, while management stood back and watched.

Black employees may get an early indication that they are being used for black-on-black crime. Betty was highly recruited to be a key player on a growing sales team. David, the hiring manager, told

Betty during the interview process that he wanted her to replace Alicia, a black female on the team. Betty didn't feel right about the situation, subsequently turning the job down. She told a friend that she "couldn't do that" to another black female because she wouldn't want anybody doing that to her. Betty had courage and character, traits that prevented her from being used as a pawn in a slimy game.

Modern House Slaves pay a price. They sacrifice their dignity, kinship, and trust with fellow blacks when they willingly participate in black-on-black crime. Sometimes, the same hand that is willing to feed them, at another black's expense, is the very hand that eventually cuts their throat. This leaves them lying in the ditch on the side of the corporate highway.

Chapter 4:

VULNERABLE SITUATION — BLACK MANAGER / WHITE DIRECT REPORTS

If a black receives a promotion in corporate America, odds are he or she will have to manage white employees. This situation can present unique problems for the black manager, who is sometimes sandwiched between white direct reports and a white manager. This is risky, since the white employees may try to leverage their cultural affinity with the black manager's boss. If the black manager is not careful, disloyal employees can use this tactic to undermine and eventually displace him.

Unfortunately, in my career, I have witnessed several coups staged by white employees. These efforts usually originate when a couple of white employees think they are more qualified than the black manager to whom they report. I have even seen white employees attempt to elicit the help of black employees to smudge the reputation of the black manager, thinking that this will give credibility to their charges. These subversive activities can impose a lot of stress on the black manager, over and above the demands of his job. I have heard extremely capable black executives say they want individual contributor roles, because of the fear of having white direct reports bypassing them to speak to upper management. Here are some examples.

Johnny was an engineer whose hard work and congenial personality won him a promotion. He worked his way up from copy technician to manager. The company believed implicitly in his abilities so it afforded him several classes in management training. He began his new job with gusto and optimism. Initially, when he assigned projects to his team, everyone was all smiles. But when Johnny tracked results and held people accountable for their deliverables, he began to run into difficulties.

- One white female on his staff complained about Johnny's management style to one of the upper-level managers.

- Martha, a white employee, was sleeping with Tom, another white employee on Johnny's team. The two of them formed an alliance against Johnny.

- A couple of the white males on his team, without consulting Johnny, would make changes to the project deliverables. Often they were late with customer data, which made Johnny look bad to his management team.

Johnny felt as if he could battle this situation. He tried to build rapport with his staff by taking them on team outings. The group enjoyed these outings, but continued the disloyal behavior. When one of his employees complained to Johnny's manager, the manager came and questioned Johnny directly. Johnny fired the employee, but that did not stop the others from going behind his back to complain to upper management. Eventually, Johnny's blood pressure skyrocketed to stroke levels, causing his doctor to place him on bed rest in the hospital. The doctor warned him that unless he changed his job, he might die from a stroke or heart attack. Unfortunately, he lived in a town with a very small black population. He didn't have a local support system, and had to rely on phone calls to relatives who had no corporate experience. Over the next couple of months, Johnny's blood pressure remained out of control, even while he was on vacation. After his management team criticized him for missing customer goals, Johnny decided to sell his house, transfer to a lower position in another region, and start over.

Meanwhile Ricardo, another black manager, was enjoying a successful career as the CEO of a small company. He had built the company from scratch and had a great track record with his customers. A much larger, electronics company recruited Ricardo to come take on a high-level position. This company felt he had the appropriate skill set to execute the management changes necessary to turn a division around.

Ricardo inherited a team of all-white males earning high salaries, each of them with long tenure at the company. Early on, Ricardo's team was eager to please. Each team member spent time courting Ricardo for his attention. A couple of them convinced Ricardo to take on a huge, risky project to gain more customers. Ricardo trusted their advice, and invested a large sum of money to launch the product. Poor planning by members of his team resulted in a rollout that was a debacle. The company's inability to respond to demand lost it favor with valued customers.

Rather than take responsibility for poor planning, Ricardo's directs tried to use him as a scapegoat. They hatched plans to get Ricardo kicked out of his role. Fortunately for Ricardo, he shared the same secretary with some of his directs. Mary, who happened to be black, had access to e-mails detailing the nasty things they were planning for Ricardo. She warned Ricardo of the underhanded plot in progress. This allowed him to plan his transition before his reputation could be damaged.

One critical piece of advice in this book is what Ricardo knew: A black employee should make friends with secretaries in the organization as if his career depended on it. Secretaries get access to information, often before the information is well known. They know or can find out the personalities of the key employees in an organization. Most importantly, they can watch your back, helping you to see knives that are coming.

Secretaries are not the only workers a black employee should befriend. Janitors in a company can be key allies. They overhear an extraordinary amount of information. Greg, a black executive, always talked to Mike, the janitor. Mike was older and told Greg that he liked to see young brothers who had made it. Greg had worked at the company for a few years and had achieved an upper-level position. Greg's office was in the executive building along with all of upper management, including Greg's boss. Mike cleaned all the offices in the building. One day when Greg was working late, Mike came by to empty his garbage cans and dust the office. Greg chatted Mike up as usual, and was in a decent mood. This changed when Mike informed Greg that he overheard Greg's manager discussing plans to displace Greg; the manager was just waiting to recruit a replacement. Greg thanked Mike for the heads-up. Greg called one of his mentors and asked him about open positions in his group. Greg arranged a transfer out of his job into his new role, all at the surprise of his manager. Without Mike's intelligence info, Greg would have been a sitting duck.

Some blacks display bourgeois arrogance when it comes to secretaries. Because these employees don't have fancy degrees, blacks sometimes underestimate their importance. Pam was Mark's secretary. He had moved from a prestigious company in New York to a large company in the West. Mark's secretary would suggest networking contacts and ideas to him. He would speak to her condescendingly, and dismiss her suggestions as silly. It turned out that a couple of his white employees were quite unhappy with the expectations that Mark had placed on them. Mark even demoted one white female direct report. Pam told Mark to spend time networking around the organization with people whom she knew had influence. Mark thought the black people he selected with impressive titles had more pull, and decided to spend his time with them. When his white employees staged a coup by complaining to his manager, Mark went from approximately fourteen-hundred employees to one, the secretary. The co-workers he had spent all his time networking with could not save him. Later, some of his closest networking contacts were forced to retire and, in the end, the only person left to support him was the secretary.

In the corporate environment, there are always people willing to do anything to get ahead. That is the reason black-on-black crime happens. Black employees who throw cultural kinship out the window in favor of gaining points with the man in charge are the perpetrators of these casualties. Even though victims of black-on-black corporate crime don't die, they can lose their livelihood as a result. This in itself is often like a slow death.

Chapter 5:

TURTLES, MAMMIES, AND OTHER LONG-TERM SURVIVORS

Unfortunately, for a lot of blacks to survive in corporate America, they must appear non-threatening to their white superiors. There are many variations of non-threatening blacks in the workplace. One of the most common is the Turtle. You know the cliché: The turtle is slow and steady, but wins the race. This is only a half-truth. A Turtle is a worker who is soft-spoken and reliable. In many performance rating systems, Turtles are referred to as "solid performers," "meets or achieved expectations," or "B players." This group of employees sometimes gets pimped, since they are doing a lot of the grunt work but don't get the highest raises or notoriety. Turtles execute their assignments on time with little fanfare, and keep moving forward. They have such an agreeable disposition that they rarely push back on their managers.

Some white managers maintain the presence of a Turtle to improve their numbers in diversity. This type of manager likes a black worker who is reliable and presents no worries. In addition, keeping the Turtle on his team allows him to feel justified when he has to get rid of a black who stands up and pushes back. When the manager dismisses the other, more vocal black employee, he does not feel guilty because he still has the Turtle around. Some companies have a term called "Coaching Up," where an employee provides legitimate critical feedback to his or her manager. In reality, "Coaching Up" often does not work too well for blacks in a corporate environment. It sometimes builds resentment in the white manager. Resentment then turns to "Coaching Down" feedback, which eventually turns into a pink slip for the black employee who complained.

Jonathan is a good example of a Turtle. He studied engineering and accepted a job on a large team under a white male manager. Coming in, Jonathan displayed a great sense of humor; he was well-liked by his manager and his teammates. Since Jonathan was smart, his manager gave him difficult assignments, which were always completed on time. However, Jonathan's manager never made him a lead on the team. The four lead spots were reserved for the manager's favorite white male direct reports.

During one of my conversations with Jonathan, he said that he liked working "under the radar." He didn't want to deal with a lot of political games, and was content with surviving the layoffs that came every six months. Jonathan made a choice to stay and continue to play the Turtle on the team. He had a daughter in college and wanted to help her financially until she graduated. What would have been the point of challenging his manager for more visible assignments? He risked alienating his manager, being laid off, and causing hardship for his child in college. Barking back at his manager could have negatively affected three lives: his, his stay-at-home wife's, and his child's. He wanted to minimize his stress and collect a safe paycheck. Can I criticize Jonathan's choice? The answer is *no*. Jonathan played a game that he could win. Like most Turtles, he was not a risk-taker and chose to stay in an environment where he was not getting his due in order to collect a steady paycheck.

Another example of a Turtle was Raymond, who also studied engineering. He received his degree from Stanford. Raymond exhibited an enviable but rare combination for an engineer: He was intellectually bright and also sociable. He completed all his assignments flawlessly. Other team members and management, who needed new, innovative ways of looking at designs, often consulted him. Nevertheless, Raymond was never promoted to be a manager of a design team. He was always the worker bee that everyone liked.

Raymond lived a modest lifestyle; he purchased a small house, attended church, and enjoyed movies. He didn't have the baggage of kids or a wife, so he had freedom to make choices. But Raymond never fought for the management position that he deserved. He didn't think the extra money and politics were worth it. Playing the Turtle role seemed to pay off for Raymond. He was content with the quality of life that he currently enjoyed. Raymond didn't want to rock the boat.

Is a black employee wrong for choosing to remain a Turtle? In reality, there are pros and cons. Yes, a Turtle operates in a safe zone; under the radar, so to speak. But what happens when a company falls on hard times and the manager has to do deep cuts on his team? People who operate under the radar are often viewed as less critical by their management, and less visible to managers of other areas. Turtles may be perceived as being less valuable than some of their vocal white counterparts. This perception can cause a manager to place the Turtle on the layoff list. Consequently, all the Turtle's loyalty and hard work are forgotten.

In addition, Turtles maintain a lot pent-up of frustration. They don't speak out when everyone around them is getting promoted. They seethe and find ways to cope. But long term, what is this doing to the Turtle's internal organs? What is this doing to the Turtle's mental health and family relationships? We all know that blacks have a higher rate of high blood pressure, heart attacks, diabetes, and other stress-related illnesses. What percentage of this group do you think are Corporate Turtles? Is it possible that some black employees survive the corporate shuffle by being Turtles, while others die a slow death from stress?

Finally, if a Turtle settles for less opportunity, he will get less. This often means these lower earnings affect his ability to save. He will have less to invest or send his kids to school. There are no guarantees in today's corporate world, so behaving like a Turtle is a financial gamble for the black employee.

Another type of black corporate survivor is the Corporate Mammy. Since the word has an ugly connotation in most black people's minds, let us talk about stereotypes in general. In reality, no matter how much we detest stereotypes, they exist because many continue to believe in them. That is a cold, hard fact. Believing in stereotypes makes some people comfortable because this allows them to predict human behavior. We have, in previous chapters, discussed how many blacks throughout history felt it was imperative to make white superiors feel comfortable. Sometimes black employees find themselves in one of two predicaments: The black employee can make superiors feel comfortable by behaving a certain way, or sometimes a white's comfort level with us is based on how we look and carry ourselves. This comfort factor is less in our control. There are certain black female employees who play into the Mammy stereotype whether they realize it or not.

As depicted in many old movies, Mammy had certain characteristics. Primarily, Mammy worked hard from sunup to sundown. She was jolly, overweight, and listened to white people's problems while offering comforting advice. She was highly religious. Until the 1970s, many whites held steadfastly to that image- to them she was a black nursemaid, a kind of comforting caricature inherited from the Deep South. Later, the Black Power movement emerged and birthed heroines like Angela Davis. Which one do you think an average white person would be more comfortable with, Hattie McDaniel's Mammy from *Gone with the Wind*, or Angela Davis?

Black women in the corporate work environment who fit the Mammy profile are women who are single, sometimes overweight, spiritual, and great listeners. Their spiritual base allows them to listen to other people's problems with a sympathetic ear. Just because employees or managers come to work does not mean they can mentally leave all their problems at home. People have problems with their kids, spouses, boyfriends, parents, dogs, cats, etc. They bring these burdens right to work. They want to talk to someone they trust. If a black female employee has Mammy characteristics, she may fall into the listening and advising role. By listening and advising, she becomes locked into the Mammy role. Don't get trapped into the Mammy role of listening to everyone's problems at work! I have seen others who have fallen into this trap, and the relationships are never mutual; you do all the listening, and they do all the talking. The black female employee should not let people use her as some kind of cheap therapist. Being an amateur therapist may feed a black female's ego, but it does not put more money in her paycheck. She should encourage her co-workers to use their insurance benefits to go see a real therapist.

Maria was a prime candidate for the Corporate Mammy stereotype. She had worked at her company twenty-plus years. She fit many characteristics of the Mammy stereotype: overweight, talkative, and eager to advise co-workers on their personal problems. She would often compliment her white male managers on how smart they were, how young they looked, how good they looked in their suits; volunteered to take their kids shopping; and served as a tour guide for relatives when they came to town.

Maria's skill set had long ago become outdated. Actually, she had only formally finished her college degree at night a few years earlier, after working several years. Why had management promoted her, even with a stale skill set? The answer was simple: She made them feel good about themselves. They trusted her. She was a non-threatening black they could admit to the inner circles.

Maria had a counterpart, Vanessa, who was Ivy League educated, slim, attractive, and full of new ideas. The division head thought she was a great hire since she had such stellar credentials. She achieved great results on her projects and built a great team. She lasted five years, until some of her white female co-workers expressed concern. They complained about her aggressiveness and access to superior white male managers. Soon after, Vanessa was let go while Maria remained.

Why was Vanessa let go and Maria retained with no fresh skills? Quite simply, Vanessa was good, perhaps a little too good. She was perceived as competition. Maria never competed with anybody. She just listened to people's problems and made them feel good.

Some corporate environments don't welcome the Corporate Mammy. These include the fashion industry, investment banks, and companies with hard-driving, pseudo-military environments. Sleek, slim, and articulate employees are the norm at these companies because they need a contemporary, youthful image to appeal to their clientele.

Although use of the term Mammy may not sound or look good in print, the reality of the matter is that Mammies are long-term survivors in the corporate structure. Why do they survive? Perhaps it is because white managers perceive them as non-threatening. Sometimes white managers can penalize black female employees if the employee doesn't fit into the Mammy stereotype. Although it is definitely taboo to espouse these stereotypes, people fall prey to them anyway. So let's be frank: Black female employees need to be aware of this stereotype or they may unknowingly become locked into this role.

One other type of black long-term corporate survivor is the Consummate Networker. These employees are charming, bright, and have top-rated skill sets. They make it a point to get to know many people outside of their department through coffee meetings and lunches. They are well-dressed, articulate, and squeaky clean. They volunteer in any company-sponsored community service efforts. In order to show a diverse employee base, some white managers will invite Consummate Networkers to attend a big event with key clients. Networkers establish alliances outside of their direct work area, a smart choice. That way, they have a parachute anytime they may need it.

One employee who had a parachute was John. He was attractive, tall, and had great presence. Because of his charm and drive, John was hired into a regional sales position. His attributes helped him gain unprecedented market share. He socialized with senior management, and was well-liked. Things were going great for John until one of the CEO's direct reports wanted to hire his college friend into John's job. Consequently, John was pushed into a job requiring a skill set he did not have. Due to his prior stellar performance, management did not understand why John could not deliver. They blamed him, stating that he had lost his motivation. However, John had an ace in the hole. A female co-worker with whom he had established an alliance had been promoted to a high-ranking position. John scheduled coffee, they had a discussion, and she hired him. John is now thriving in his new position and having fun to boot. He is an example of how establishing a powerful network of alliances can bulletproof your career.

We all make choices to suit our lifestyle. Electing to be a long-term survivor is a choice some black employees make. The black employee needs to assess the cost of making that choice. These costs can include such compromises as slower promotions, slower bonuses, and less recognition compared to their white counterparts. Once employees have weighed the costs and the benefits of these options, they can make the appropriate choice for themselves.

Chapter 6:

TIGERS, TESTOSTERONE, AND TERRITORY — BLACK MALES / WHITE MALES WORKING TOGETHER

As evidenced by the world's history of war, men from different cultures have always fought over territory to establish dominance in order to utilize natural resources. The corporate work turf is no different. Traditionally, white males have dominated the management ranks in big business. However, due to progress in affirmative action and education, blacks have penetrated the environment of most companies in the Fortune 500. Black males competing against white males for raises and promotions have become more commonplace. White males often perceive affirmative action as a threat, giving a less-qualified candidate equal or better job positioning. Such perceptions can be a problem for us, and here is why.

The theory of Social Darwinism proposed by Herbert Spencer holds that in any environment, the fittest members will survive and flourish while the weaker members should be allowed to die.

Throughout history, this theory was used not only to justify war but also colonialism. The Think Quest Web site puts it best, "Colonialism was seen as natural and inevitable, and given justification through Social Darwinian ethics – people saw natives as being weaker and more unfit to survive, and therefore felt justified in seizing land and resources."

Unfortunately, the performance rating and succession planning systems many companies have put in place fuel the "survival of the fittest" behavior. These systems force a manager to list his employees in order of importance. The high-ranking employees get the best raises and bonuses, and the lowest-ranked ones are targeted for downsizing. These systems by their very nature will force competition between team members to become the manager's pick. This can promote ugly and desperate behavior to get the top ratings and incentives.

In most corporate environments, people size each other up. I had one co-worker say in a matter-of-fact way that when he walked into a meeting as a new employee, he looked around the room to see who he could backstab and take out. Sometimes, those doing the sizing up will make assumptions because you are black. They may think that you do not have powerful political contacts established, or that you are less experienced. If an employee is viewed as weaker, even if it is not true, the games of discredit may begin. If the employee is lucky, he detects this early and is able to combat it by working hard to prove himself. If the employee does not detect this, his reputation may be damaged by subversive comments from teammates and business partners.

This seems like aggressive, callous behavior, and it is. A tenuous work situation may develop when a black male is working for a white male. The conflict heightens when the black male becomes part of a team, competing for his manager's favor. This may involve team members discrediting him to make themselves look good. If a black male is perceived as more vulnerable, then he is more open to attack. This will require him to expend energy defending himself as well as continuing to do his job well.

These aggressors also have an advantage. They may have more in common with the white manager and his lifestyle than the black male does. This gives his co-workers an advantage that he does not have. Consequently, he has to figure out early how to work around this disadvantage.

Let's focus on prevention. The first step in prevention is identifying potential failures. The following are three critical mistakes black males make when working for a white male:

1. Outshining the manager. This occurs when a black male worker receiving accolades from co-workers becomes threatening to his manager.

2. Allowing frustration to mount, causing the black male to debate with his manager. There is a fine line between sharing viewpoints and irritating the manager.

3. Relying solely on politics or hard work, but not both.

Let's talk about Mistake Number One. This is one of the things our ancestors realized from slavery, yet many educated blacks don't comprehend. A black male must make whoever is in charge of his destiny feel comfortable with him. Blacks often joke among themselves about how they have to behave in a non-threatening manner for whites to accept them. The word "threatening" can have many meanings. It's not just being perceived as violent or militant; the black male can also be threatening by appearing more successful. Almost all corporate blacks know how to maintain even-keel emotions. Sometimes they may even mask emotions in the work environment. This allows corporate blacks to reduce their chances of victimization in the workplace. However, the threat of a black male appearing more capable than his manager is often a threat that he doesn't acknowledge. In <u>The 48 Laws of Power</u>, Robert Greene writes:

> Never Outshine The Master. Always make those above you feel comfortably superior. In your desire to please and impress them, do not go too far in displaying your talents or you might accomplish the opposite — inspire fear and insecurity.

This is especially true when it comes to a black male. He should strive to do a great job while vigorously promoting his manager's abilities. If the manager hears from his colleagues the black male is praising him, he will allow the black male to continue working and share opportunities as they arise. If the manager feels insecure in the black male's shadow, the black male can count the number of days before he receives unfounded criticism or a pink slip.

Mistake Number Two is simple, yet headstrong black males don't get it. As long as the black male works for the manager, the manager is in charge. The manager determines the black male's performance ratings and compensation. Black females fall into this trap less often. They are often socialized to take a secondary position in a family or religious setting if there are male authority figures present. If the black male provides hard data for a contradictory opinion as opposed to arguments based on emotion, management may be more easily persuaded. It is still management's choice to accept or reject the black male's advice. The manager's department is his domain, and he rules it. If the black male becomes adamant about his position, the manager may form a negative opinion. The manager will knock the black male down a notch the first change he gets. If the black male continues to argue with his manager, the black male may be subject to the next round of layoffs.

How much of a disadvantage is it for a black male to have grown up without a father figure at home? If the black male employee did come from this background, how uncomfortable will he be with a male authority figure telling him what to do on a day-to-day basis? Unfortunately, single-parent households have become more and more common among African Americans. For example, the 2000 census figures show 46.2 percent of African American children live in single parent families vs. 17.7 percent of non-Hispanic white children. In another instance, the U.S. Department of Health and Human Services' African American Healthy Marriage Initiative notes that "Children in two parent households are less than half as likely to have emotional and behavioral problems as children in single parent households." Is it possible that these two statistics might support the idea that black males may have a harder time working with an authority figure in corporate America?

Is it possible that this will also mean that if a single mother catered to the black male, he may have a sense of entitlement? This possible sense of entitlement might not integrate well in an environment where a black male has very little power. I've seen black males crippled by expectations of entitlement, resulting in being fired from job after job. For the purposes of this discussion, entitlement will be defined as "expecting to get preferential treatment." If a black male has a white male manager, the manager controls the black male's earning potential and ability to pay his bills. The black male must always keep in mind that his destiny is controlled largely by his manager. Even if the manager likes the black male employee, he often has to do a hard sell to his white colleagues to acquire promotional opportunities for the employee. Unfortunately, the reality of the matter is that if the black employee's white peers have issues of racism, this could effectively halt his opportunities for promotion.

Unlike a father who bonds to his son for life, the manager can cut the cord at any time. Take Bill, for example. A hardworking single mother, Ruth, raised him and his brother. Ruth wanted to build confidence in her sons, since their father was absent from their life, by raising them to believe they could accomplish anything. She often confronted people when she felt that either of her sons was being treated unfairly. They both attended top schools and received graduate degrees. Bill became an engineer, and David opened up a law practice. Bill got a job at a well-respected technology company. At first, he performed well on the job. Later, however, a pattern developed. He would get a job, would work for a while, disagree with his manager, and then get laid off. Bill would always think he was justified in his opinions. What he failed to realize is that he was dependent on these managers for his income. The confidence and the unwillingness to negotiate instilled by his mother actually worked against him in relationships with white male managers.

Mistake Number Three is one I have seen quite often, especially in black professional organizations. Let's talk about politicking. Establishing a strong political network is important. Successful blacks have coached me that you need two different types of mentors: a black mentor and a white mentor. We run to black networking meetings and latch on to the few successful blacks who are there. They are already overburdened with several people clinging to them for career advice. There is something people fail to realize: *A black male should be working just as hard to get a white mentor as he does a black one.* I've heard black males complaining that they work harder than everyone else but don't get promoted. Getting promoted is just as much political as it is results-based. You have to be both well-known and well-liked to have your name thrown into the promotion hat. Then guess what? Most of the people sitting around the table deciding who is going to receive the limited promotions for the given year are white males. A white mentor can turn a black male on to opportunities that will get him better known by his white peers. Ken Chenault, CEO of American Express, is a classic example of this. He was groomed by the former AMEX chairman, Harvey Golub. Ken was bright, articulate, and hardworking, but that would not have been enough. His CEO made the difference in his career by helping Ken gain access to opportunities even when others were placing roadblocks before him. Obtaining a white mentor is a critical move.

41

Without one, Ken may have been a solid, unknown worker in the corner forever.

We just talked about how important schmoozing is, but it is not sufficient on its own. The black male is going to have to show hard work and tangible results. The black male is often judged by a combination of what results he has produced and by how he is perceived. This is especially true with the affirmative-action cloud hanging over the black male's head, which can cast doubt about his abilities in a white manager's mind. Some black males rely on working the black networks. However, many of the mentors in these groups are in danger themselves. I have seen situations where the mentors even rely on their tutees for advice and access to information. Often, the black mentors have been burned by the system, and have become lame ducks. The other side of this scenario is the black mentors who can help the black male navigate the corporate maze with greater ease. You need a black mentor, but sometimes their ability to help the black male advance is limited.

Black males can lose sight of the fact that their skill set needs to be kept current and in high demand. If the black male's skill set is stale, the best white male mentor may feel it is too difficult to help him. In addition, a black employee's lack of competitive skills may make it difficult for the manager to qualify the employee for opportunities in other organizations. With a competitive skill set, a black male can more likely be used to fill a need. Developing that skill set is the black male's responsibility. One way to learn about what skills are in demand is to check the company's online job postings. Another way to learn about perspective job opportunities is to check Monster.

com, a website that can verify which skill sets are broader than your company's needs.

Case in point, if a black employee develops a skill set that is specific to his company, he may be limiting his opportunities with other corporations. One other option is to talk to a human resources specialist at the company. The human resources specialist can provide information regarding future job openings. If there is an area of interest, schedule an appointment with the hiring manager to discuss how to get the skill set required. One way to gain experience for advancement is to take a transitional position at a lower level in order to learn new skills. Top-notch skill sets increase an employee's chances for promotional opportunities.

The skill sets of politics, good mentoring, and knowing when to cut losses and move to a more fertile environment are just as important as education. Education means very little after a candidate has been hired. The following points summarize how black males can position themselves to get ahead:

1. Career advancement does not always require changing jobs. Realize who is in charge. Schedule time with your manager as often as possible. This will allow him to get to know you better, track your progress, and feel comfortable promoting you. Find opportunities to speak well of your manager to his colleagues; this creates a win-win situation.

2. Recruit an influential white mentor as if your life depended on it. Find out what data or work is

important to him and see if you can help him out on a couple of his projects. If you are taking his highly compensated time away from his job to talk to you, there has to be something of value you are providing him as well.

3. Don't get in the habit of pushing back with your manager. If you do, you need to look for another job or open up your own business.

4. Keep your skill set current. If you have not taken a class or obtained a certification in two years, you have a stale skill set and are less valuable.

5. If you are spoiled, leave the demands on what you deserve at home with your mama! Unless she is cutting your paycheck, you have a new authority figure you have to take orders from now.

Bottom line, black males have to work strategically. Once you get frustrated and your emotions take over, you are done. In today's workplace, acquiring a current skill set is equally as important as gaining favor with your manager.

Chapter 7:

BLACK SISTERS WORKING WITH WHITE SISTERS

I am a regular reader of *Essence* magazine. In March 1998, I picked up a copy. The opening of an article detailing a panel discussion with white women and black women grabbed my attention:

> *Black and white women: what still divides us?* — includes a related article on coping as a Black woman in the office — Panel Discussion

> *Essence* March 1998 by Audrey Edwards and Dana Canedy

> "What's the first thing you think of when I say 'white women'?"

> Intelligent

Funny

Manipulative

Privileged

"And what's the first thing you think of when I say 'black women'?"

Strong

Determined

Attitude

I thought — finally, somebody is discussing this uncomfortable topic. My friends and I have talked about this for years among ourselves, but we had never seen it formally discussed anywhere. I went on to read the article; it had candid dialogue about black women's perceptions of white women and vice versa. The article gives us an opportunity to examine the responses to the opening question: "What's the first thing you think when I say 'white women'?" The answers of "manipulative" and "privileged" were strong, negative words used by the black female participants. What do they mean by "manipulative"? There is an unspoken perception shared by some black women that black females can't do certain things that white women can get away with, such as working from home, taking extended time off to take care of a sick child, long maternity leaves with the assurance that your job will be there upon return, and pet duty.

One of my black friends, Lucille once told me, "Jane and Allison both planned to go out on extended maternity leave and got promotions announced before they left. They get to come back from caring for their child to even bigger jobs. I stay here and slave along with the rest of us, and we can't even hope to get a promotion."

I had another friend say, "Susie wasn't feeling good the last two months of her pregnancy, so her manager let her work from home the rest of the time until she had the baby. We have to work till the water breaks." I had another friend named Charlene who said, "My white female co-worker said she had to leave early because her cat fell off the table last night and he wasn't feeling well. You let me, a black woman, say that to my white manager and see the response I get."

Are white women manipulative at work? Some may use their feminine wiles to get breaks while others do not, but the response from the black females on this panel lets you know that is their definite perception based on their work experience.

One situation involving manipulation includes white women working as part of a team and reporting to a white male manager. My friend Laurie put it this way: "My teammate can go in and whine to my manager about why she should get a bigger job even though her work is weak. He listened to her and promoted her because she's young and blond. I've done ten more projects than she has this year, but I didn't get promoted." The sad thing about Laurie's statement is that it may be true, but it is difficult to prove. The way most of us try to solve this situation is to either work harder or change groups.

Let us explore the black panelists' comment regarding white women being privileged. Why do black women have this perception about white women? One reason is that white women are more likely to be married to high-earning spouses. This allows them to live in neighborhoods and join country clubs where they have homes that are more comfortable and greater chances to network with other affluent people. In addition, white women are more likely to be born into a family of affluence compared to black women. As mentioned previously in the Introduction, black household net worth is significantly lower than white household net worth.

One friend, let's call her Susan, said, "When Constance bought her house, her father gave her the 20 percent down payment. When I bought my house, I had to save for two years to come up with the down payment."

Another area of privilege is exposure. Many professional whites grew up in a house where the mother, father, or both were successful professionals. This may have afforded the childhood benefits of taking exotic trips or attending private schools. As children, most of my black professional friends never traveled to Europe or outside of the U.S. Most of my white professional female counterparts share stories of traveling abroad with their parents. The word "privileged" can translate into black women thinking that white women have an advantage by just being born white. This advantage is said to help them succeed in the workplace.

Now let's examine the word "attitude" used by the white female participants. When anyone comments that black women have attitude, it is often thought of as negative. The perception is that black women are difficult and unpleasant to work around. If white women come into the workplace with this perception, it will take very little to reinforce this opinion. I've heard black people say that they can't freely express their opinion or demand actions from their co-workers because they don't want to be viewed as aggressive. Often, we will stay quiet even when we should speak up, for fear of being labeled. Television has reinforced the thought that black women have attitude, through characters in TV shows including *Jerry Springer*, *Good Times*, and *The Jeffersons*.

In my opinion, white male managers are often naive about blending women of different races into the work environment. *The Wall Street Journal* featured an article in May 2006 titled, "Differences Are Emerging Among Women Employees." This article speaks about how older female managers have negative perceptions of young women fresh out of school and vice versa. If women of different generations have problems, what happens when you throw race into the mix? A past manager has told me that I should make nice with an impossible female co-worker. He said, "Why don't the two of you women just sit down and talk? Maybe go out together for drinks after work. You should be able to find something in common." I think most white male managers feel that black and white women should be able to work well together because they have the "woman" thing in common. They may have visions of us talking about our kids and sharing recipes. However, other characteristics women have in common sometimes surface: pettiness, jealousy, and jockeying for position with a male superior.

How do black women succeed in this game? The ones I observed have three things in common. The first is impeccable control over their emotions. Even when their buttons are pushed, they maintain a calm and soothing demeanor at work. It's hard for people to argue with a calm person. Sometimes when women have the reputation of appearing composed, it is difficult for people to believe any lies told about them. This may also create a perception that the black female employee is more capable and serious. If a black female employee loses her temper, she may risk the possibility of someone using her emotional outburst against her. For example, she could express her disagreement about a business plan in an angry tone as opposed to expressing the same idea in a conversational tone. However, the idea she intends to communicate may be used against her simply because she has not displayed a controlled demeanor.

One of my old co-workers, Ellen, was the epitome of collected composure at work. Her voice was always even-keel no matter what stress was being introduced into the fast-paced environment. One of Ellen's white co-workers gave her a compliment: "Whenever you come into the room and speak, you have such a calming influence." Ellen was articulate, soft-spoken, and very tactical in her approach. She kept meticulous records and when questioned, could always whip out the deliverables with the execution dates attached. Many times, she prevented herself from being used as a scapegoat by her insecure co-workers, because she could always produce the facts. To top it off, she was well-dressed, and built loyal relationships with her management based on respect for her thoroughness.

The second characteristic successful black women have is achieving and documenting results on their projects. They use this as hard evidence to combat any discrediting games played by their female co-workers. Sometimes, you may need a white male superior to come to your aid. One thing white male executives tend to focus on are bottom-line results. If a black female employee can impress her superiors and assist them in meeting their performance goals, the superiors will take up the sword in her behalf.

Take Pam, for example. When she held a meeting, she quickly got everyone to agree upon team roles, deliverables, and timelines. She could shut a whiner or complainer down in a minute. This kept her from being bogged down with saboteurs. Her teams always delivered their result on time, and management loved her for it. She will probably never be CEO, but she will always have a job because management needs her ability to execute difficult assignments.

In another scenario, one of my friends was interviewing for a sales job with a regional manager, Rick, in the Southeast. He introduced her to his staff, and when he got to Katrina, he said, "She is my top producer and a single mother. She is my most valuable team member." Katrina will get to stay around because she produces results, bottom line. Let's talk cheese: If Katrina couldn't produce, Rick would replace her in a minute. As long as the cow produces milk, the farmer will keep her around.

A third characteristic of successful black female employees is avoiding lengthy discussions about their personal life. They may reveal a few things, but they keep many things private. They seldom give potential enemies information that other female co-workers might feel jealous about, such as cars, shopping sprees, vacations, dating, etc. Consequently, the successful black female employee may be perceived as boring and non-threatening.

I once attended a function where all a high-level white executive could talk about was his black co-worker Charlene's shiny new Porsche. The black employee was very accomplished, but the executive kept coming back to Charlene's car. If he had never seen it, he would not have displayed his thinly disguised envy. Instead, he would have focused more on Charlene's stellar merger and acquisition credentials. Some blacks I know do what we call "Hide the Ride." They have a work car and a play car. They drive a less flashy car to work so as not to rouse jealousy with their white co-workers. They save the luxury "play" car for socializing and personal trips.

Black females in a white environment can feel as if they are walking a tightrope. If they are aggressive, they become threatening. If they are passive, they are viewed as ineffective. If they move too far either way, they plummet to their corporate death. They may often end up masking many emotions to survive. Eventually, many blacks fall off the tightrope. They get tired of masking their emotions and explode. Could this be why we have a higher rate of stress-related illness than the general populace?

In today's corporate environment, most black females will work with or report to a white female somewhere during their career. The black female employee should acknowledge that the dynamics between women of different races can be challenging, though it can be managed by using some of the tools we have discussed. However, if she experiences bad chemistry with a white female manager who has high-level political alliances, she should move on to greener pastures before she suffers any permanent career damage.

Chapter 8:

IVY LEAGUE START / UNEMPLOYMENT FINISH — DEGREES DON'T GUARANTEE SUCCESS

Historically, black families sometimes have put too much emphasis on education as our ticket out of poverty. This is a result of post-slavery denial of our right to education. After the civil-rights movement, more blacks were able to go to college, receiving government funding to get advanced degrees. Education is often required as a ticket of entry into the workplace for higher-level corporate jobs. Entire generations of blacks were encouraged to pursue higher education as a way to guarantee success.

However, the educational advancements we make come with some downsides in the contemporary workplace. Let's discuss a few examples in which advanced education actually worked against a black employee.

A few blacks have had the privilege of obtaining degrees from Ivy League institutions. An Ivy League stamp will make a resume stand out from the slush pile. Many people associate prestige and hard work with an Ivy League education. These schools are highly selective, and a student usually has to have unique qualities to be accepted. Unfortunately, being labeled "special" by your manager and co-workers because of your education does not always have the desired benefits of shooting you up the corporate ladder.

A young man we'll call Michael Watson graduated from Harvard Law School. One of the largest law firms in San Francisco heavily recruited him. Michael finally felt rewarded for all the long hours of studying when he received his written job offer at a nice starting salary. The new job would be the first step in paying off the huge college loans he had accumulated while in graduate school.

The law partners welcomed Michael with open arms. They were pleased to get him on board, since it was rare to find an African American with his stellar credentials. However, he was expected to pay his dues just like everyone else in the law firm.

Several of his classmates were also hired by the law firm. Unfortunately, he was one of the few, if not the only, black from his class who was hired. Everyone knew that the California bar was one of the toughest in the country; it was coming up. He had to put in long hours both at work and studying for the bar. This caused Michael to operate on very little sleep. His body became depleted of energy. For support, he talked to his mother on a weekly basis; she just kept telling him how proud she was of him.

Michael passed the bar. Since being hired, he had gained a reputation as a thorough researcher — though ironically, he was never elected to be in charge of high-profile cases. He worked long hours attempting to prove that he was qualified to lead a big case. He saw his white counterparts being promoted around him. He thought the answer was to work even harder. Michael began to survive on very little sleep. The partners kept promising that he was due to get a promotion soon, but it never happened. Michael began to worry about his superiors' perception of his work performance. He questioned why his white counterparts were climbing the corporate ladder at his expense. To top it off, he had huge loans that would be difficult to pay off unless he was promoted to a higher salary grade. Whenever he consulted with his mother, she continued to say she was proud of him; his day would come. Unfortunately, his mother couldn't give him the money to pay off his loans. She actually borrowed money from Michael to help pay her bills. He started to feel as though his ability to advance was hanging by a thread. Eventually stress, disappointment, and tension mounted until Michael's breaking point resulted in suicide.

This is a tragic story of someone who seemed destined for success, but who ended up being crushed against the glass ceiling. What could have saved a talented brother like Michael?

First, he needed a support system. People who actually listened, and could relate to his plight. Unfortunately, the more hours Michael worked, the harder it became for him to build a support network. He needed quality relationships to overcome the pressure and plummeting self-esteem. The moral of this story is that Michael made the mistake of giving all his time and energy to his employers. He should have given them a hard day's work, but not all his spare time and thoughts.

If Michael had developed a professional support network, he would have been able to build alliances with other black professionals. A peer might have been able to ease Michael's desperation. Black professionals fare better in the corporate workplace when they have access to the support of others who have similar qualifications and aspirations. This would have helped Michael scrutinize his environment more.

Second, it would have helped Michael to contact any other blacks who left the firm. This would have allowed him to explore other options outside of the one that was strangling him. At a minimum, he needed an experienced black lawyer as a mentor.

Third, students are increasingly leaving school burdened with student loans. Some students with advanced degrees may find themselves in over a hundred thousand dollars' worth of debt. It can be daunting for anyone to thrive under such a financial burden. But there are options, such as taking jobs that have forgiveness benefits. These jobs will usually require a commitment to serve an under-represented section of the population. In turn, the organization will pay off the loan, or allow it to be written off. Loan deferments allowing six months of breathing room are another option. Ivy League and private schools may be prestigious, but students need to look at two things: the subsequent debt coming out of these schools, and the return on investment. Pedigree education at the expense of quality of life is an unacceptable trade-off.

Some of us use school as a place to run from the unfairness of the workplace. Carl planned to flee his job to attend graduate school. After completing his undergraduate degree, he worked at a large corporation for a while. He then decided to return to graduate school.

Carl was accepted by a top-five MBA program. Armed with a nice shiny MBA, he was hired by one of the largest companies in the U.S. He worked marathon hours, but unfortunately, management overlooked him for promotions. He decided to try his hand at another major corporation. He eventually landed a job at a top financial institution. He rose quickly, because he had the right black package: clean-cut, bright, and soft-spoken. A successful white mentor took him under his wing. The mentor promoted Carl to a huge regional manager position. Carl felt like he had escaped the New Jersey slums of his childhood. He never felt guilty about his success, because he had earned his rightful place as an executive.

In a year, due to a major merger, he transferred to another site seeking more opportunity. Unfortunately, he lost his huge management responsibility. To make matters worse, his mentor, who had been so fair to him, was being forced to retire. Carl was demoted from working in a prestigious office to confinement in a cube. He applied to other jobs that were worthy of his background. The new change of guard did not give him the opportunity. Co-workers began making snide remarks and questioning his ability. His days became longer and painfully unpleasant. He pursued outside interests such as studying Spanish and traveling. However, it was not enough to deal with the stagnant, frustrating environment at work.

Like many blacks, Carl thought the answer was running to get more education. He decided to go to a private university for an advanced degree in international studies. This degree would put him at least fifty thousand dollars more in debt, with no guarantee of a better salary. A lot of us use school and multiple degrees to flee a bad situation and start over. But what price do we pay? Degrees do not guarantee access to the good ol' boys network. A combination of politics, a powerful mentor, and education are required to open the doors toward advancement.

At forty-two years old, what should Carl do? He could try to get an international assignment with his current company. This would give him real-time experience in the business world abroad, without incurring life-altering debt. If his current company won't facilitate the change, he should seek the same type of opportunity elsewhere. After a certain age, school is no place to run and hide. Carl needs to assess and act if his current company doesn't appreciate his worth. There is always the option for Carl to transition from a job to running his own business, where he would have control over his paycheck and self-worth.

Some of us learn early from our mistakes. We are able to rebound with smart decisions. Tina was able to use what she learned in college and life to free herself. Frustrated with her job, she decided to pursue an MBA at the University of Pennsylvania. During the admissions process, Tina was led to expect multiple job offers upon graduation. Tina studied, earned high grades, and was optimistic about her earning potential. Unfortunately, at graduation, there was a recession. With a dry job market, she had difficulty finding a job worthy of her degree. She searched for two years, but received no offers. To make ends meet, she settled for a thirty–thousand-dollar-a-year job at a phone service center. With a one-hundred-thousand-dollar student loan debt, Tina was ill-equipped to make adequate payments. How did Tina recover from the hole that she dug herself into? She studied real estate in her spare time, with a future goal of selling rehab properties. She obtained financing by leveraging her good credit, eventually investing in several properties. Tina realized that corporate America and education were not her ticket to success. Belief in herself and managing her resources proved to be her way out.

Education opens many doors in corporate America. We are often encouraged to earn graduate degrees from top schools. We are led to believe these degrees will make us more competitive in the job market. However, education does not guarantee success. Many blacks with great educational backgrounds never get promoted to executive positions. What should their strategy have been?

> **Solution:** Selecting the right mentor and knowing when to cut your losses and move to a more fertile environment are just as important as education. Once you hit the door as a new hire, where you earned your degree means very little. Here are five ways to survive and thrive in corporate America:

- Focus on building a good peer network. Obtain information from other departments on opportunities and growth trends.

- Get a good black mentor, inside or outside your company, with experience in your field. Make sure the mentor is someone you can feel safe confiding in. Once you have carefully selected a mentor who relates to your growing pains, he can give you tactical advice on your next steps.

- Make sure you have a good work/life balance. Build hobbies and relationships outside of your work environment. This is critical to prevent burnout.

- Be open to less glamorous ways to pay back your student loans. This may mean working for an underserved population, or for a nonprofit that has loan forgiveness benefits.

- Always have multiple streams of income in your mind. The minute you walk in the door, you should be strategizing. Work to funnel the money you make from your paycheck to other investment opportunities or businesses. Don't wait till you are in trouble to do so. Subscribe to *Inc.* magazine and *The Wall Street Journal.* These are two of the best sources for tips on trends in business.

You must use a combination of these strategies to put the odds of success in your favor.

Chapter 9:

CUBS IN THE WILDERNESS — NEW AFRICAN AMERICAN GRADS

New grads are often excited about their new jobs and nice salaries. It's a heady time for many African American students who finally obtain their degree after struggling to finance their education for many years. However, prior to accepting jobs, or soon thereafter, new grads need to make a priority of establishing a surrogate family.

What is a surrogate family? It's a group of people who provide emotional support, friendship, and possibly comfort in times of trouble, even though they are not biologically related to you. Some new grads established their first surrogate families while in college, where most students feel alone after being shipped off to this new environment. They are between phases—on the one hand, they are no longer young children and, on the other hand, they are not yet full adults.

They often join churches where a local family "adopts" them. Some college students also form surrogate families with classmates in their dorm or their field of study.

When you become a young professional, the need for a surrogate family diminishes, but if you accept a job outside your hometown, you will be leaving behind your primary family of parents and/or siblings. Young professionals need allies for support and companionship.

When you take your first job, everything seems great. Many experienced professionals call this the "honeymoon phase." It usually lasts about three months but it can vary widely in length. When the honeymoon is over, difficulties are bound to arise. New grads need a support system outside their job to validate them if they experience any erosion of their confidence from the politics at work.

So, how do you choose surrogate family members? You can contact local organizations for information on attending their meetings. Examples of good target organizations are local chapters of the Urban League and alumni chapters of black professional organizations, including National Society of Black Engineers, National Black MBA, and 100 Black Men.

African Americans usually try to find a church home in their new city. This should be part of your strategy for building a surrogate family but not your only resource. Some churches are looking for young, fresh members who are open to volunteering on several committees. Young professionals need to participate, but should neither spread themselves too thin nor expect to receive much practical support in return. A good church would be one with proactive members in the community at large. An excellent church boasts a membership of many professionals with whom one can enjoy fellowship; members' varied levels of income and business accomplishments add value to the fresh-out's experiences.

Be careful of using co-workers for surrogate family members. Spend time getting to know a potential surrogate family member and his or her ethics before divulging any personal information or insecurities. If a co-worker shares your private struggles with others in your work environment, it could be detrimental to your current job and future career options. New grads should seek certain behavioral characteristics in potential surrogate family members. Choose people who are kind, not judgmental. This way, you will feel open to share your vulnerabilities with them. Also, choose people who are wise, strategic thinkers and not just doers.

Surrogate families can help you understand the community and patterns of discrimination and crime in the city, as well as the quality of neighborhoods and schools in your area. They can also share their personal networks to help grow your support base.

In the October 2000 edition of *The Black Collegian*, Bob Johnson, founder of BET, said, "All business is personal, so make friends before you need them." This wise advice also applies to relationships with surrogate families. Create them before you need them.

Chapter 10:

TOP DOG OR TALKER

Today, there's a lot of talk about becoming an entrepreneur among black professionals who have grown weary of their corporate jobs. It has become trendy for professionals to say they want to run their own business. The question is: Do they have what it takes? First, let's look at the definition of an entrepreneur as given by Wikepedia on August 26, 2007:

> An entrepreneur (a <u>loanword</u> from <u>French</u> introduced and first defined by the Irish economist <u>Richard Cantillon</u>) is a person who undertakes and operates a new <u>enterprise</u> or <u>venture</u> and assumes some accountability for the inherent risks. A female entrepreneur is sometimes referred to as an entrepreneuse.

The new and modern view on entrepreneurial talent is a person who takes the risks involved to undertake a business venture. In doing so, they are said to efficiently and effectively use the <u>factors of production</u>. That is land (natural resources), labour (human input into production using available resources) and capital (any type of equipment used in production i.e. machinery). A business that can efficiently manage this and in the long-run hopefully expand (future prospects of larger firms and businesses) will become successful.

To get a business off the ground, a person has to work hard and procure the resources necessary for that particular venture. What are the minimum characteristics you need to enter the elite club of entrepreneurs?

1) Positive Attitude: Most people would say they have a positive attitude, but there is a key indicator as to whether this is fact or fiction.

   Negative friends and family. Most future entrepreneurs spend their spare time learning, reading, or talking to people who are encouraging them to move ahead with their dream. Does this sound like you? Or, do you spend a lot of your spare time listening to negative friends who only complain about their current circumstances at work, but don't take major action to change their situation? Do you have friends who gossip about what "so and so's husband is doing" or who had "messed up hair" at a party or function?

These types of friends and family fall into the negative category. They waste both their time and yours by endlessly criticizing and gossiping about others. The more you are around that negative energy, the less positive energy you will have to pursue something for yourself. Who you associate with is probably the most critical factor in becoming an entrepreneur. If it is family members who are being negative, and it is unrealistic to eliminate them from your life, minimize what you tell them so that they have no idea what you are working on until it's completed.

If you are serious about your dream, cut negative people out of your life as fast as you can and replace them with helpful folks you can learn from. Also, if so-called friends spend their spare time criticizing people, they will eventually spread their negativity to you and your dream. Michael Baisden uses a special term for these folks on his radio show: dream killers. A dream is a gift from God to fulfill a purpose He has for you. Don't allow anyone to kill it. Every minute wasted with negative people is one less minute spent on building your future.

2) Associating with Other Entrepreneurs: Find a way to hang around other business owners.

Talk to friends or family members who have already started their own business. Ask them if they will spend extra time with you.

Contact SCORE, an organization of retired executives who offer business advice in your local area. Its Web address is www.score.org.

Contact the National Association of Women Business Owners (NAWBO), which has nationwide local chapters that meet and plan activities. Its Web site is www.nawbo.org.

A mentor. If you talk to most business owners, you'll find they had someone to show them the ropes. Angle to get an entrepreneur as a mentor. Warren Buffett had a professor who mentored him and taught him value investing. He later went to work for this professor. The rest is history. If Warren Buffett needed a mentor, so do you. You can ask around at church to see if any members own a successful business. Approach these people, get to know them, and then explain about the business you are trying to get up and running. Because you are both church members, they may be more inclined to help you. If you don't belong to a church or can't find one that is suitable, talk to your service providers—such as your hairdresser, barber, or lawn service agent—to see if any of them would consider mentoring or guiding you.

3) Super-strong Work Ethic: Most of us work hard at our corporate jobs. But to get a business up and running, you are talking about work on an entirely different level. Do you have the family lifestyle to support this?

Are you willing to sacrifice some social time to get your venture off the ground?

Tom Joyner is probably the most well known and successful DJ among African Americans. He has the moniker of the "Hardest-Working Man in Show Business." In the early days, he flew back and forth between Dallas and Chicago to do radio shows in both cities. He had a superhuman work ethic. The result? He became the most successful African American in his field.

Sean "P. Diddy" Combs is a highly successful entrepreneur in the music, perfume, and fashion industry. Few people know that to make his dream come true, he was willing to take the train every day from Washington, D.C., to New York to intern at a record company while attending Howard University. All people see is how successful he is today; they do not see the extreme sacrifices he had to make to position himself in the early days.

It is a well-known fact that many businesses fail within the first two years. Lessen your odds of joining that group by making sure you have the basic criteria for becoming an entrepreneur. If you don't have these characteristics, work on obtaining them. Then you may be positioned to launch your business with the odds of success stacked more in your favor.

Chapter 11:

INEPT NETWORKING SKILLS — UNDERSTANDING QUID PRO QUO

These are the words I most dread hearing at a social function: *"Can you get me job where you work?"*

This all-out assault makes me feel exploited. The person does not have to take the time to get to know me before he or she hits me up. Sadly, a lot of us feel comfortable asking people for jobs in the first couple of minutes of conversation.

When a lot of us think of networking, we have visions of going to a function, talking to a high-level manager, and getting a job. We expect the hook-up. Expecting to get something for nothing is what I call inept networking. The hook-up has no place in networking, as successful people do not operate this way. They operate by using a modernized barter system that basically says, I can offer this to you for that. George Bush Sr. used the more eloquent term *quid pro quo.*

Are you an inept networker? Here are some inept networking strategies that may cripple black professionals:

Inept Scenario Number 1: *Going to coffee with a new manager you don't know.* Coffee is too short a time to talk about anything constructive. The manager may spend too much of his time trying to get to know the black employee, then coffee is soon over. The employee may or may not have a chance to follow-up and get more of the prospective manager's time.

Inept Scenario Number 2: *Picking an articulate black mentor solely because he has an impressive title.* An impressive title may be a relic from an earlier heyday. The executive's influence may have waned due to a demotion or a shift in corporate culture. Often, an employee keeps the previous title even if he or she has less power and responsibility in the new role.

Inept Scenario Number 3: *Meeting a contact at a networking function and asking for a job up-front.* This personally irritates me. If I just met you, I don't know you or your work ethic. Why would I recommend someone I don't know and put my reputation at stake?

Inept Scenario Number 4: *Not networking with people on your level.* This type of networking is often overlooked. I have gotten some of my best information on upcoming organizational changes and intelligence from my peers in different divisions. If you form the right peer network, you can inform each other of open jobs in your division. This is especially important if one of you gets in trouble in your area and needs to be rescued.

Inept Scenario Number 5: *Not researching your prospect first.* People can talk impressively, but you need to find out what is the general consensus on this person's influence before investing a lot of time — that is, unless you are just looking for a new friend or drinking buddy.

Inept Scenario Number 6: *Spending time and energy networking with too many groups, and not shoring up the relationship with the direct manager.* He is the one who decides the black employee's immediate future, and cannot be left out of the picture.

When you deal with accomplished businesspeople, you can't expect something for nothing. They didn't get to where they are by giving, giving, giving. Usually, they give their time and resources to get something of value in return. If you are networking with these people, you have to give them something of use. One of my co-workers, Colita, would photocopy articles from the *Harvard Business Review* and forward them interoffice to an executive for whom she used to work. She would always include a hand-written note saying, "I thought you might be interested in this." She is a consummate networker, and always knows how to keep relationships warm even when she doesn't interact with a person frequently.

Thomas Stanley, author of the ground-breaking books The Millionaire Next Door and Networking with the Affluent, says:

> High-performance networkers gain endorsements for reasons that go beyond the basic product or service they offer. They do extraordinary things. For example, many enhance the revenues of prospects. In other

words, they sell the prospects' products. They give this help before asking prospects to become clients. The affluent will go out of their way to endorse you if you do extraordinary things for them.

Stanley is saying that you have to impress by giving before influential people will feel comfortable enough to endorse you. This is the opposite of the hook-up mentality. You have to spend time researching what is important to the manager you want to influence. Maybe he needs data. Maybe he needs help with a project. Maybe he needs you to introduce him to someone else who can be of service to him. There are many ways to provide value to an executive. You can also talk to people who work for him to see what his biggest goals of the year are, and brainstorm as to how you can help. I know one high-level executive who requires people to do some project work for him as a prerequisite to considering them for a position.

George Fraser, the African American networking guru, says that you can network with someone by making a connection through asking questions:

> When you ask good questions, it's easier to make a connection and establish common ground (people, places, and things). Additionally, people are clear about the purpose of your networking. People also enjoy the verbal engagement and the sharing and the exchange of interesting and meaningful information. Remember, the more common ground you establish, the higher the trust level; the higher the trust level, the

more willingness a person has to share key contacts, private information and important resources.

Good questions indicate interest and concern about what is important to a potential prospect. This gives him a chance to highlight his achievements and desires. This also indicates what the networker needs to focus upon. Basically, networking comes down to *quid pro quo*. When the networker provides help, most likely the prospect will want to reciprocate.

When a previous employer hired me, I was welcomed by a black executive who offered to meet with me. He asked me questions and found out I was new to both the company and the area. He arranged for me to meet with other high-level executives he was friendly with. He also knew that I was hired as a specialist in my field, and he would need my coaching on a project. To his credit, he knew how to network, because after meeting all the contacts he set me up with, I was more than willing to go the extra mile coaching him.

Internal networking groups are good vehicles for building rapport with individuals in other divisions. These networking groups have interesting company speakers who can provide information on where the company is headed. However, these groups are seldom the best place for high-powered networking. One reason why they are not a good place for networking is that there are so many individuals competing for the speaker's attention.

Now let's focus on black professional organizations. These groups provide a great way to meet peers from other corporations and to discover which of these companies are expanding and hiring.

However, these groups are ineffective if a large portion of their membership is at the same professional level. I have also seen in the past that if they have immature people running them, they can turn into social clubs and dating services.

One of the ultimate — but, unfortunately, costly — ways to network is by joining a city club or a country club. City clubs are located in major urban areas. They provide a way for businesspeople to network and dine in a comfortable environment. Memberships can be obtained by way of referrals. City clubs often have a membership roster filled with the town's movers and shakers in business. Gaining membership into a country club requires a different process. A prospect usually has to be invited, and the fees are much higher. However, country clubs provide exclusive access to business owners and community leaders, and that is why white Americans formed them in the first place. To gain optimal enjoyment, people should first make sure they feel comfortable in the environment. Country-club members are often invited to parties, business presentations, golf tournaments, etc. These all provide great arenas to broaden networking contacts. If you can afford it, I highly recommend taking advantage of this opportunity.

There are many ways to network. The key to good networking is providing something of value to potential prospects. Remember, there is no such thing as a free lunch.

Chapter 12:

NO DRINKING, NO GOLF, TOO MANY VACATIONS, AND OTHER FAUX PAS

Many factors come into play in the workplace. There is a percentage of each day where the employee actually does work. There is also a percentage of the day that is spent in conversation with co-workers. Sometimes these conversations may extend to out-of-work activities. Over the years, there are mistakes that blacks make at work that actually have nothing to do with work. Let's discuss some common examples.

Sooner or later, a black employee will be asked to attend an after-work get-together such as a happy hour. Most blacks dread these invitations, due to their fatigue from dealing with co-workers all day. The black employee may spend many hours a day discussing and listening to topics that culturally don't matter to him. Phony conversations all day can take their toll. Sometimes, when a black employee receives an invitation to socialize after work, he may be tempted to turn it down because he would prefer to go home and shed his corporate façade. This is a critical mistake. No matter how tired I am, I always go out to these functions, because each time I attend, I hear a piece of information I would not have been privy to if I had gone home. Going out for drinks with co-workers should be factored into a black employee's to-do list just like a key project deliverable or training session. Blacks who are fundamentalists will say, "But I don't drink." Well, if you don't drink, just order a Coke or iced tea. Black employees can still go out and be part of the group. Discussions that occur on these outings often reveal little-known office politics or possible organizational changes. Frequently, if he doesn't show up, the black employee becomes the subject of drunken dialogue at these get-togethers. Robert Green, author of <u>The 48 Laws of Power</u> says this about isolation:

> Do not build a fortress to protect yourself — isolation is dangerous. The world is dangerous and enemies are everywhere — everyone has to protect themselves. A fortress seems safest. But isolation exposes you to more dangers than it protects you from — it cuts you off from valuable information, it makes you conspicuous and an easy target. Better to circulate among people, find allies, and mingle. You are shielded from your enemies by the crowd.

Some white co-workers feel more comfortable with a black employee if they can socialize with him or her away from work. They feel like they can get to know what's behind the work mask. They often use these opportunities to learn details about your family, interests, and educational background. I've heard blacks make comments like,

"White people ask too many questions," or "They are being nosey." How much should be revealed at these out-with-the-gang discussions? Common sense comes into play here. Unfortunately, common sense is something some educated blacks seem to think they need less of in the corporate environment. If a black employee senses that revealing the truth about his out-of-work lifestyle will incite jealousy, he should reveal as little as possible. Competitiveness can come into play when a black employee says he lives in a certain neighborhood, kids go to private schools, or he has expensive hobbies. These things may make some co-workers feel jealous if the black employee is perceived as having a better quality of life. Once the jealousy is created, some of the white co-workers may subconsciously try to sabotage the black employee. Advice for socializing after work: A black employee must listen more than he talks. He must also avoid drinking too much.

Vacations are a necessity; they provide a much-needed break from the stress of work. Growing up, blacks may not have been able to enjoy vacations due to the limited income of their parents. Today, black professionals with disposable income have broadened their vacation travel to include places such as Europe, the Caribbean, South America, Alaska, and Australia. Exotic places are fun to see, but as with any good thing, there are drawbacks. In order for a black employee to leave for a vacation, he has to request time off from work to set up coverage while he is gone. The black employee gets the obvious question, "Where are you going for vacation?" His answer is key here, and may have unexpected consequences. For example, whether he says "I'm taking my wife to Fiji," versus "I'm going to see my family in Georgia." Which response do you think will be more non-threatening to an insecure white manager or co-worker? Be careful here. Remember what Jack Nicholson said to Tom Cruise in the movie *A Few Good Men*: "You can't handle the truth." When the black employee discusses travels to exciting places, he may think he is sounding impressive. But what he may actually be doing is stirring up envy. The black employee needs to be discerning about how much he reveals. Discretion is something that should be in the black employee's toolkit for survival.

One person who was not good at using discretion was Candy. As a child, she became accustomed to taking extended family vacations to Europe. When she took time off from her job to travel to the South of France, she let her manager know details on her vacation plans. Subsequently, every time she asked for time off in the future, her manager would ask sarcastically, "What exotic place are we off to now?" His tone was an indicator of his resentment that Candy was able to travel to a place he admitted he had never been. When it came time for raises, do you think the manager's perception of her expensive travels played a part in the small raise he doled out? Maybe; maybe not.

Every corporate environment I've worked in has scheduled golf outings. The more men in a corporate environment, the more likely this is to happen. I'm going to be frank here. Just as the black employee invested in his education, he should invest in a set of golf clubs and lessons. Why do I feel so strongly about this? Golf is a bonding event that teams use to get away from the office. Just like at happy hour, office politics are discussed on the golf course. Actually, you spend a longer time playing a round of golf than you would drinking after work, which allows more time for talking and networking. The following is what Donald Trump said about golf in his book, <u>How to Get Rich</u>:

I made a lot of money on the golf course before I
ever went into golf as a business. I found solutions
to problems, new ideas for ventures, and even a new
career.

Golf teaches subtle things about someone's attitudes and behavior,
since it is such a difficult game. The game reveals if someone has a
bad temper or is unsportsmanlike. If someone is good at golf, it can
be an indicator of his or her networking ability and influence. The
better the golfer, the better a networking contact they may be.

Non-athletic black females pay a price when it comes to golf outings.
They often miss the bonding aspect of the game. They whine about
not being able to play, instead of doing something about it. This gives
their white co-workers the impression that black females are different
and don't fit in. They are viewed as limited and not fun.

Black females often use, "I've never played before," or "I'm not that
good," as an excuse. Based on my experience, most people who work a
nine-to-five job are not that good at golf. They don't have time to play,
practice, or improve their game. This includes most white co-workers
as well, unless they belong to a club, live on a golf course, or played
college golf. Black females should not take the easy way out, giving
work comrades an excuse to exclude them in future outings.

Socializing with co-workers can be a minefield for the black employee.
Participation without too much personal disclosure is a fine line that
the black employee has to walk. When in doubt on what to talk
about, ask a trusted black peer or black mentor. They can share their
thoughts to help you discern what to disclose.

Chapter 13:

UGLY SITUATIONS / NO WAY OUT — A FINAL WORD

Apart from all the other scenarios described in this book, there are some ugly situations that cannot be overcome no matter how you look at them or try to justify them. Eventually, you will have to face the reality that there may be no way out. How do you know when to cut your losses and move on? Here's a checklist to review.

As you read on, ask yourself if you fit into one of these categories:

- Bad performance review

- Demoted by a powerful manager

- Had repetitive arguments with your manager

- Put on a performance improvement plan

- Assigned junk projects

- Victim of multiple complaints from co-workers to management

If any one of these categories applies to you, you are no longer hanging by a thread, the cord has been severed. Update your resume pronto. There is no need for lengthy discussion or rationale. The reality of a dead-end situation calls for drastic action. Cut your losses and move to safer ground.

CONCLUSION

Due to inappropriate career choices, many super-qualified black professionals are stuck in the wastelands of corporate America. Not only are they often hanging by a thread, they are often caught in that predicament because they don't know how or when to make the right move. One of the problems these professionals might encounter is navigating the chess games of politics and subtle racism in corporate America. One wrong move can jeopardize their career and livelihood. Older relatives can usually offer little support since the sophistication of the games has increased over the past couple of decades. Many black professionals flounder, with little or no support from anyone.

However, education and training allow black professionals to have greater options. The more options they have, the greater their chances are for success. The intent of this book has been to discuss realistic solutions to difficult situations that black employees encounter. Hopefully, moving forward, the black professionals will not have to feel like there are no strategies for handling uncomfortable work situations.

Perhaps one or more of the chapters in this book will be applicable to many commonly experienced situations. Prior to reading this book, part of the problem for many black professionals may have been denial about sticky situations in the work environment. Many may have been naive regarding the dangers they are actually facing. A prevailing thought might have been, "No, this can't be happening to me. I've dotted all the I's and crossed all the T's by going to school and working hard." But if a treacherous situation presents itself in the workplace, the sooner a black employee acknowledges it and acts, the better off he will be. I hope that this book will be used as a reference when a difficult work situation presents itself.

If you find this book useful, I encourage you to give it to others, especially newly minted African American college graduates. I wish I had known some of these lessons in the beginning of my career versus halfway through.

The success of this book ultimately depends on how helpful this material proves to you. My hope is that the advice herein can save at least one black employee from some of the stress that I have experienced while meandering solo through the corporate maze.

I wish you much success in plotting your next move!

Printed in the United States
105167LV00003B/172-219/P

9 781434 326935